Mega-Funny
Math Poems & Problems

23 Fun-to-Read Story Poems with Worksheets That Teach Multiplication, Division, Measurement, & More!

by Dan Greenberg

SCHOLASTIC
PROFESSIONAL BOOKS

New York • Toronto • London • Auckland • Sydney • Mexico City • New Delhi • Hong Kong

Cover design by Jaime Lucero and Norma Ortiz

Cover and interior illustrations by Rick Brown

Interior design by Ellen Matlach Hassell
for Boultinghouse & Boultinghouse, Inc.

ISBN 0-590-18735-X

Printed in the U.S.A.

Contents

Introduction 5
Topics Chart 7
Meet Ruthie and Max 9

COMPUTATION

The Ice Cream Shop 10
The Great Card Castle Disaster 12
Square Dance Sing-Along Jubilee. 14
Bug City 16
Max's Talent Show 18

GEOMETRY, PATTERNS, AND TIME

Ruth's Mystery Garden 20
The Tooth 22
Ruth's Fantastical Zoo 24
The Snowball 26
Suds. 28

FRACTIONS AND DECIMALS

Zeke and Zack 30
The Six Days of Summer Vacation. 32
Why? 34
TV Guide. 36
Soup's On 38
Morrie's Thanksgiving Tale 40
The Deci-Mater 42
Playing Percentages 44

PROBLEM SOLVING

Bicycle Max 46
Hoop Dreams 48
King for a Day 50
Max and the Millions 52
Dear Max 54

Answers 57

Introduction

Welcome to *Mega-Funny Math Poems & Problems*.
Before going any farther, here's a message from Max and Ruthie.

A Note From Max and Ruth

Hello, we're Max and Ruth.
Is your math class sometimes boring?
Are your problems sort of tedious?
Do your students end up snoring?

Do you want math to be fun?
Then by all means take a look
At the mathematical POEMS
On the pages of this book!

They're dedicated to the proposition
(And some may find it radical)
That a poem can be entertaining
And still be mathematical!

So if you like your poems
With a dash of mathematical truth,
Then by all means check us out!
Sincerely, Max and Ruth.

If Max and Ruth are familiar to you, you
may remember them on **Scholastic.com,**

Scholastic's Internet Web site. Max and
Ruth were so popular that they now have
their own book! On these pages you will
find 23 poems dedicated to Max and
Ruth's proposition that poems can be fun
and mathematical at the same time. Put
another way, these math problems are
"pure poetry."

So, you can relax—you're in good
hands, both mathematically and other-
wise. The problems in this book make a
wide variety of mathematical topics
accessible to students. They focus on
using mathematical concepts in real-life
situations—a key element in the National
Council of Teachers of Mathematics
Curriculum Standards.

Organization
There are 23 poems in the book. Each
poem is introduced by Max or Ruth and
focuses on one of the following mathematical topics:

Computation covers basic operations,
number facts, patterns, number sense,
and problem solving.

Geometry, Patterns, and Time covers sorting, geometrical shapes, calendar and
time problems, and critical-thinking skills.

Fractions and Decimals covers modeling,
basic fraction and decimal concepts, computation, percents, and solving problems
using fractions and decimals.

Problem Solving covers critical thinking, logical reasoning, estimation, number sense, and problem-solving skills in a variety of different contexts.

The final problem for each poem presents a Super Challenge, which stretches the concepts that students have used and allows them to apply those concepts in new ways. The problems become increasingly difficult as you progress through each section of the book. The final section, "Problem Solving," contains the most challenging problems.

The Solutions

Annotated solutions to each problem are presented on pages 57 to 62.

Using the Poems

All the poems are intended to be read aloud, but they should delight and edify students no matter how they encounter them.

- Read the poems aloud or have volunteers read them.

- Have partners or small groups work together to reread the poems and solve the problems.

- You may need to have students use extra paper to solve some of the problems.

- Assign poems to individuals for high-interest, self-paced study.

- Use the poems as part of an interdisciplinary program to combine literature, poetry, and other topics with math.

Teaching Tips

Math is part of your world. Use the poems to emphasize that math and mathematical reasoning are not isolated skills separate from everyday life. Use the poems as an opportunity to show how the math grows out of the situation presented.

There is more than one way to solve a problem. Most poems contain a variety of problems. Some are computational. Others focus on logic and reasoning skills. Still others combine problem solving with computation. Stress that students can use any method that works to solve a problem. Encourage them to use creative thinking.

A starting point. Use the poems to stimulate enrichment activities for all students. For example, students may:

- compose new problems for the poem.

- compose new poetry verses to extend the poem.

- use the poem as a springboard to create their own poems.

- create illustrations, diagrams, and charts based on the poem.

- put on plays, skits, or other productions based on the poem.

Most important, use this book to make math fun for students. Show them that in some situations, they can have their mathematical cake and eat it too.

—*Dan Greenberg* (for Max and Ruth)

Topics Chart

Use this chart to select reproducible pages that will fit
the individual needs of each student in your class.

POEM	PAGE	MATHEMATICAL SKILLS
COMPUTATION		
The Ice Cream Shop	10	Counting, Adding and Subtracting Money Amounts, Making Change, Basic Facts, Number Patterns
The Great Card Castle	12	Basic Addition Facts, Number Patterns
Square Dance Sing-Along Jubilee	14	Addition, Subtraction, Multiplication, Division
Bug City	16	Solving Problems With Facts and 2-Digit Numbers
Max's Talent Show	18	Solving Problems With Facts and 2-Digit Numbers
GEOMETRY, PATTERNS, AND TIME		
Ruth's Mystery Garden	20	Sorting, Logical Reasoning
The Tooth	22	Patterns, Logical Reasoning
Ruth's Fantastical Zoo	24	Geometry, Shapes
The Snowball	26	Time, Elapsed Time
Suds	28	Using a Calendar
FRACTIONS AND DECIMALS		
Zeke and Zack	30	Modeling Fractions
The Six Days of Summer Vacation	32	Modeling Fractions
Why?	34	Equivalent Fractions, Adding Fractions, Ordering Fractions
TV Guide	36	Adding, Subtracting, and Multiplying Fractions and Whole Numbers
Soup's On!	38	Measurment, Using Fractions
Morrie's Thanksgiving Tale	40	Adding, Subtracting, and Ordering Fractions
The Deci-Mator	42	Multiplying and Dividing Decimals
Playing Percentages	44	Percents
PROBLEM SOLVING		
Bicycle Max	46	Using a Map
Hoop Dreams	48	Using Discrete Numbers
King for a Day	50	Choosing the Operation, Estimation
Max and the Millions	52	Choosing the Operation, Number Sense, Estimation, Logical Reasoning
Dear Max	54	Multistep Problems, Logical Reasoning, Choosing the Operation

Meet Ruthie and Max

Hello, my name is Ruth,
And this young man is Max.
Does math make you nervous?
Sit down then and relax.

Sit down, take your shoes off,
And give yourself a look
At the mathematical POEMS
On the pages in this book.

Our poems are each handcrafted
And especially designed
To tickle the tip of your funny bone
And stimulate your mind.

Our poems have fractions, decimals,
Word problems, and number facts.
They're written by two friends
Named Ruthie and Max.

The Ice Cream Shop

My name is Max, and this is the truth.
I'm nine and a half, and my best friend is Ruth.
We like to eat ice cream, so sometimes we stop
At a place we call Beekman's Soft Ice Cream Shop.

Now we were at Beekman's, old Ruthie and me,
We stood there and Beekman said, "What'll it be?"
I said, "We'll have a Slurkie—no, make it a Smushee
With peanuts on top—and not a bit mushy.

"And then while you're at it, here's what to do:
Drown it in chocolatey caramel goo.
Pour on butterscotch syrup and other good stuff,
Then dump on a bucket of marshmallow fluff.

"Then add sarsaparilla and wild cherry flavor,
And, oh, while you're at it, could you do us one favor?
Top it off with whipped cream and some green Jujubees.
That's what we want, could you make us that, please?"

Well, old Mr. Beekman, he looked sort of funny.
Then he turned and he said: "*You got any money?*"
"Money?" we said. Then we reached in our jeans
And pulled out 2 quarters and 5 jelly beans,
Three nickels, 2 dimes, and a Barbie doll shoe
Plus 8 shiny pennies, then we asked, "Will this do?"

"*Will this do?*" he repeated. "Well I don't mean to holler,
But the Smushee you want costs exactly one dollar.
So count up your money, yes, that would be nice.
And make very sure, 'cause one dollar's my price."

Mega-Funny Math Poems & Problems   Scholastic Professional Books

Name _____

The Ice Cream Shop

So now can you help us? Do we have enough
To buy that big Smushee with all that good stuff?
So count up our money. Don't make a mistake.
'Cause we're getting really hungry,
And we don't like to wait.

SOLVE If you need more space, use a second sheet of paper.

1. How much money do Max and Ruthie have in quarters? In dimes? In nickels? In pennies?

_____

_____

2. How much money do they have in all?

_____

3. Do they have enough money to buy the Smushee? If not, how much more money do they need?

_____

4. Suppose Ruth finds another dime in her pocket. How much money will they have?

_____

5. Including the extra dime in problem 4, how much more than one dollar do Max and Ruth now have?

_____

6. An ice cream cone costs 79¢. How much change would you get if you bought a cone with a dollar bill?

_____

7. What coins would you need to have exactly enough to buy a 79¢ ice cream cone?

_____

8. How many dollar bills would you need to buy two 79¢ ice cream cones? How much change would you receive?

_____

SUPER CHALLENGE Ruth used 3 quarters to buy a 59¢ mini-cone and got 20¢ in change. Did Ruth receive too much or too little change? What should she do?

_____

_____

_____

Counting • Adding and Subtracting Money Amounts • Making Change • Basic Facts • Number Patterns   **11**

The Great Card Castle Disaster

It began this way on a cold rainy day—
The house seemed dark with gloom.
This much was true, there was nothing to do.
Then Max said, "Let's build a fort in your room!"

After a quick bowl of cereal,
We gathered material
And laid decks of cards on the floor.
And in just over an hour,
We built a card tower
That reached to the top of the door.

But we didn't stop there,
We stood on a chair,
Got out more decks and kept dealing.
We moved through the halls
And kept adding walls
Until our card castle reached to the ceiling.

We kept adding cards
Out into the yard
Till we'd built a gigantic skyscraper.
We kept going faster
Until the disaster—
Remember, this was all made of paper!

When Ruthie's dog Rover
Knocked the thing over,
All 14 floors crashed to the dirt.
The thing hit the ground
With a dreadful sound,
Thank goodness that no one was hurt!

Mega-Funny Math Poems & Problems   Scholastic Professional Books

Name _____

The Great Card Castle Disaster

Now that it's gone,
We look out on the lawn
And think of rebuilding our tower.
If we each built seven floors,
No fewer, no more,
We'd finish in less than an hour.

But as you may have guessed,
While this might seem best,
There are other ways to add to 14.
So here's what to do:
Think of a few
And write them for Max and me.

SOLVE

1. Write ALL the addition combinations involving two numbers that have a sum of 14. There are 8 combinations in all. Use the table.

2. Find all the ways to add up to the other numbers in the table. Fill in the table. Some numbers are given.

NUMBER	WAYS TO ADD	TOTAL NUMBER OF WAYS
10	10 + 0, 9 + 1, 8 + 2, 7 + 3, 6 + 4, 5 + 5	6
11		
12		
13		
14	14 + 0	8
15		
16		
17		
18		

SUPER CHALLENGE What pattern do you see in the table?

_____

_____

Square Dance Sing-Along Jubilee

Hello everyone, my name is Ruth,
I'm your host for the big Jubilee!
If you like to compute and holler and hoot,
Then this is the place you should be.

1. Swing your partner
   Six times 'round.
   Add four more,
   Then fall to the ground.
   Let's hear the total
   With an oinking sound:
   > OINK! OINK! OINK! OINK! OINK!
   > OINK! OINK! OINK! OINK! OINK!

2. Stomp your foot
   Eleven times on the floor.
   Take five away,
   Then think of the score.
   Then make a lion—
   Show the difference with a roar:
   > ROAR! ROAR! ROAR!
   > ROAR! ROAR! ROAR!

3. Clap your hands
   Four times in the air.
   Multiply by three,
   Then circle your chair.
   Show your total by
   Growling like a bear:
   > GRRR! GRRR! GRRR! GRRR! GRRR! GRRR!
   > GRRR! GRRR! GRRR! GRRR! GRRR! GRRR!

4. Flap your arms
   Thirty times like a duck.
   Divide by six—
   Go ahead, good luck.
   Honk out the answer
   Like a garbage truck:
   > HONK! HONK! HONK! HONK! HONK!

5. Hop twenty-seven times
   Like an elevator.
   Divide by three,
   Then spin like a skater.
   Yodel out the answer
   In the voice of a fourth grader:
   > YODEL! YODEL! YODEL!
   > YODEL! YODEL! YODEL!
   > YODEL! YODEL! YODEL!

Mega-Funny Math Poems & Problems   Scholastic Professional Books

Square Dance Sing-Along Jubilee

Make up a verse
To this song, okay?
Add, subtract, multiply,
Or divide right away.
Don't wait until tomorrow,
Do it today!
TODAY! TODAY! TODAY! TODAY! TODAY! TODAY!

SOLVE If you need more space, use a second sheet of paper.

1. Here is an addition sentence for the first verse: **6 + 4 = ?** What number will complete the sentence?

_____

2. Write a number sentence for verse 2. How many times do you roar?

_____

3. Replace the numbers in verse 2 with different numbers. Then write a new number sentence for the new verse. How many times do you roar now?

_____

4. Replace the numbers in verse 3 with different numbers. Then write a number sentence for the new verse. How many times do you clap now?

_____

5. Change the number 6 in verse 1 to a two-digit number. How many times do you oink now?

_____

6. In verse 5, change the number 27 to 36. Think of a different one-digit number that will divide evenly into 36. How many times do you yodel now?

_____

SUPER CHALLENGE Write your own verse for the poem. Use addition or subtraction. Then write a number sentence to show what happens in your verse.

_____

_____

_____

_____

_____

_____

_____

_____

_____

Bug City

Hi, I'm Ruth, this is Max,
Can you guess what we found?
We were digging in the yard
Near the fence, underground.

We found 48 bugs
Under some rocks.
So we brought them all home
In a plastic bug box.

They're squirmy and icky,
They scatter and scoot.
My mom thinks they're awful,
But we think they're cute.

We put them in jars
And gave them all names,
Like Samantha, Melissa,
Sparky, and James.

Some of them fly.
Some of them squirm.
One has no legs,
I think it's a worm.

Now this is what happened,
Why my mom got so cross.
Twelve bugs escaped,
Twelve others got lost.

We found James in the basement,
Samantha under a curtain.
The rest will turn up,
Of that we are certain.

And if we don't find them
(And we haven't, so far),
I know they'll be happy
Wherever they are.

Mega-Funny Math Poems & Problems Scholastic Professional Books

Name _____

Bug City

Whether you like bugs,
Yes or no,
Solve the problems
You see below.

SOLVE If you need more space, use a second sheet of paper.

1. Ruth and Max put all 48 bugs in a plastic bug box. How many bugs escaped or got lost?

_____

2. How many bugs were left in the plastic bug box in problem 1?

_____

3. In all, Ruth and Max found 3 bugs in the basement and 5 under the curtain. How many bugs were still missing?

_____

4. Ruth and Max put the bugs they found in problem 3 back in the box. How many bugs were in the box now?

_____

5. Each of the bugs that Ruth found in the basement and under the curtain has 6 legs. How many legs do these bugs have in all?

_____

6. Five of the bugs that are still lost have 6 legs each. How many legs do the five bugs have in all?

_____

7. Ruth divided all the bugs in the box in problem 4 into 4 groups with the same number of bugs. How many bugs were in each group?

_____

8. Suppose Ruth finds all but 3 of the missing bugs. How many bugs will she then have in all?

_____

SUPER CHALLENGE Twelve bugs are in a bug box. Each day 3 bugs escape. Each night, one bug returns. At what point will the box contain no bugs at all?

_____

_____

_____

Solving Problems With Facts and 2-Digit Numbers   **17**

Max's Talent Show

My name is Max,
And what do you know?
I'm working on my act
For Max's Talent Show.

Here's what I'll do
While dangling from a rope.
I'll juggle 17 balls
And tell a knock-knock joke.

Knock! Knock! Who's there?
Twelve scorpions in my shoe!
And now, with one eye closed,
I'll type a letter to Betty-Lou.

But that's not enough—
I'll build a model car
While skiing down a mountain
And playing my guitar.

Still not amazed?
Well, this is no fib.
I'll break 36 Olympic records
While wearing a baby bib!

And to top it all off,
The ultimate grand finale—
I'll sing "The Star-Spangled Banner"
With two mice named Pete and Sally.

Mega-Funny Math Poems & Problems Scholastic Professional Books

COMPUTATION

Max's Talent Show

So that's this year's Talent Show—
I hope you catch my acts.
If not, good luck, wherever you go,
Sincerely, your friend Max.

SOLVE If you need more space, use a second sheet of paper.

1. Max juggled a total of 17 red and blue balls while dangling from a rope. Nine of the balls were red. The rest of the balls were blue. How many balls were blue?

_____

2. Max had 12 scorpions in his left shoe. If he divides the scorpions into 4 groups with the same number of scorpions, how many will be in each group?

_____

3. Max broke 36 Olympic records while wearing a baby bib. He received a 3-ounce gold medal for each record. How many ounces of gold did he have in all?

_____

4. The song "On Top of Old Smoky" has 7 verses. Max sang the song over and over. In all, he sang 84 verses. How many times did he sing the complete song?

_____

5. The ski judges gave Max scores of 8, 9, 8, 6, 10, and 7 for his ski performance. How close to 50 did he get?

_____

6. What was Max's average score in problem 5?

_____

7. The owner of the Talent Club offered Max $25 per show to do his act. If Max performs 2 shows a night, how much money will he make in a week?

_____

8. One week Max missed some shows. He made only $275. How many shows did he miss?

_____

SUPER CHALLENGE Max's show was so successful that he was offered a raise. Should he take $35 per show or a flat fee of $500? Explain your answer on the back of this page.

Mega-Funny Math Poems & Problems   Scholastic Professional Books

Ruth's Mystery Garden

My name is Ruth, and here is a mystery:
Why are my hands all grimy and blistery?
Why am I muddy right up to my shirt?
Read on and you'll learn why I'm covered with dirt.

You see, Max and I, on the Fourth of July,
Found a packet of what looked like beads.
"Not at all," Max cried, when we looked inside,
"These are giant fruit and vegetable seeds."

And sure enough, when we planted the stuff,
Strange things started to bloom.
There were enormous potatoes, tremendous tomatoes,
And bananas that filled up a room.

There were huge nectarines, baseball-sized beans,
And plums like beach balls, dark red.
If you think that's scary, we had a strawberry
As big as an elephant's head!

We had green sugar peas that came up to my knees
And hot peppers up to my shoulders.
We grew oranges with peels the size of bike wheels,
And our pumpkins were as big as small boulders.

And that's not all: When summer turned to fall
And our crops began to get ripe,
We got boxes and bins, to sort them all in—
By color, shape, size, and type.

Mega-Funny Math Poems & Problems   Scholastic Professional Books

Name _____

Ruth's Mystery Garden

So here's the scoop: Sort them in groups
By color, shape, size, or kind.
Just follow your hunches, sort them in bunches,
And keep track of whatever you find.

SOLVE Answer these problems on a separate sheet of paper.

1. Sort the fruits and vegetables by color. How many groups do you have? Which fruits and vegetables are in each group?

2. Sort fruits and vegetables by shape. Explain how you sorted them.

3. Think of another way to sort the fruits and vegetables. What is it? How many groups do you have when you sort this way? Which fruits and vegetables are in each group?

4. Ruth sorted the fruits and vegetables by taste. Which fruits and vegetables belong to the "sweet" group? Which belong to the "nonsweet" group? Make a graph to show your results.

5. Max sorted the fruits and vegetables by how well they roll. Which fruits and vegetables belong to the "straight roller" group? Which belong to the "crooked roller" group? Which do not roll at all?

6. Think of a way to sort the fruits and vegetables by the letters in their names. Show how you sorted them.

7. Sort the fruits and vegetables by the number of letters in their names. Show how you sorted them.

8. Compare your groups with a classmate's groups. Are your groups the same? Why or why not?

SUPER CHALLENGE Make up a sorting problem of your own. Trade problems with a friend and solve.

Sorting • Logical Reasoning

The Tooth

It was a dark and spooky night,
And out there on the street,
Happy kids were ringing bells
And shouting "Trick or Treat!"

I was stuck inside my room,
Without a thing to do.
I had a fever of a hundred and one,
I was sick in bed with the flu.

Looking out the window,
If you want to know the truth,
Only one girl's costume caught my eye—
She was dressed up as The Tooth.

Her bag was filled with candy,
Jammed right up to the top.
But The Tooth just kept on going,
The Tooth just would not stop.

And as the night grew later,
The streets began to thin.
But The Tooth just kept on going,
The Tooth would not go in.

Finally, at the door,
I heard a frightful knock.
Good grief, I must've been dozing,
It was almost twelve o'clock!

Then The Tooth came toward me,
I shook in fright and fear.
Good grief, I thought, was this the end?
As The Tooth came ever near.

Then The Tooth tore off her mask,
And now I knew the truth.
"Good grief!" she cried, "It's only me!"
It was my best friend Ruth!

And now I saw how wrong I'd been
As the fever cleared my head.
The Tooth got all that candy for ME—
'Cause I was sick in bed.

Mega-Funny Math Poems & Problems Scholastic Professional Books

Name _____

The Tooth

If you're not from Mars
And you're not from Saturn,
Take a look at these candies.
Do you see a pattern?

SOLVE If you need more space, use a second sheet of paper.

1. What candy comes next in this pattern? What 2 candies come after that? Draw them.

_____

2. What are the next 3 candies in this pattern? The next 6? Draw them.

_____

_____

3. Make up a pattern that uses jelly beans and peppermints. Draw your pattern.

4. Draw a pattern that uses kisses, lollipops, and peppermints.

5. How would you describe this pattern in words? What are the next four candies in the pattern?

_____

6. Make up a pattern that uses all four candies. Draw your pattern.

7. Where do you see a mistake in this pattern? How would you correct the mistake?

_____

_____

8. Look at the pattern below. How many jelly beans would you put in Row 4? In Row 5?

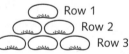

_____

_____

SUPER CHALLENGE Find the next number in this number pattern:

1 3 7 15 31 63 ?

_____

Mega-Funny Math Poems & Problems Scholastic Professional Books

Ruth's Fantastical Zoo

Welcome to the Fantastical Zoo
I'm Ruth, your Fantastical Keeper.
In my zoo, you'll find every kind
Of fantastical crawler and creeper.

Just take, for example, one single sample
Of animals from our cages.
Your eyes will feast on critters and beasts
You'll see in no other picture book pages.

In Cage 1-A, we have on display
A Square-Haired Round-Headed Furkle.
It has a clump of red hair, shaped in a square,
And a head that's round as a circle.

Over here you can see, in Cage 2-D,
A Rectangular Baby-Sitting Bore.
This rectangular critter is a great baby-sitter,
But it tends to doze off and snore.

Right now take a view, in Cage 3-Q,
Of this family of Fighting Blue Yovals.
These battling brutes wear triangular boots
And have bodies that are shaped like ovals.

And now look beyond the goldfish pond
At the Bouncing Basketball Jandles.
They come from Mars and are shaped like stars,
And play basketball in hot-orange sandals.

Over here you'll observe, around the next curve,
The Chuckling Noodle-Eating Churts.
These diamond-shaped blobs eat pasta like slobs
And wipe greasy paws on their shirts.

Square-Haired
Round-Headed Furkle

Rectangular
Baby-Sitting Bore

FIGHTING
Blue Yovals

Bouncing
Basketball
Jandles

Mega-Funny Math Poems & Problems Scholastic Professional Books

Name _____

Ruth's Fantastical Zoo

So now that you've viewed my Fantastical Zoo,
It's time to show what you saw.
At the very least, make a sketch of each beast,
So get out your crayons and draw.

SOLVE If you need more space, use a second sheet of paper.

1. Make a sketch of a Square-Haired Round-Headed Furkle.

2. Draw a Rectangular Baby-Sitting Bore. Use at least four rectangles.

3. Draw a family of three Fighting Blue Yovals. How many ovals did you draw? How many triangles?

4. Draw an entire team of five Bouncing Basketball Jandles. You can use either five- or six-pointed stars.

5. Chuckling Noodle-Eating Churts have triangle-shaped mouths and square ears. Draw a Churt.

6. A Churt ate two different pasta shapes: triangles and trapezoids. Draw a picture to show that trapezoids are just triangles with their "tops" cut off.

7. The Furkle lives in a cage that's shaped like a parallelogram. Draw the Furkle's cage.

8. Draw an animal using at least one of each shape: square, rectangle, triangle, star, circle, oval, trapezoid, parallelogram.

SUPER CHALLENGE

I am a four-sided figure. My two longer sides are equal. My shorter two sides are also equal. I contain no right angles. A line connects two of my corners, creating two identical triangles. Draw my picture.

Mega-Funny Math Poems & Problems   Scholastic Professional Books

The Snowball

I made three wonderful snowballs,
They were big and smooth and round.
And when I threw one at a tree,
It made this snowball sound:
BLAP!

I took the second snowball
And tossed it in the air.
And when it almost hit Ruth's head,
She said: KNOCK IT OFF OVER THERE!
STOP!

"I'm sorry," I said to Ruthie.
She looked at me, cold as a fish.
So I gave her my third snowball,
And she put it on a dish:
CLINK!

This happened at 9 in the morning
And this was how I felt:
I wondered, would our snowball last all day?
I wondered, would it melt?
OH, NO!

But one hour later there it was
At 10, when we came back.
We'd played a game of hide-and-seek
And now we needed a snack:
YUM!

We came to see our snowball
One and three-quarter hours later.
It seemed smaller, but there it sat
Right next to the refrigerator:
HUMMMMMM!

After that we read a storybook
And took Ruth's dog on a walk.
The next time we saw our snowball,
It was 8 past 3 o'clock.
IT WAS SHRINKING!

We played monster games until 5:11,
Then decided to go back out.
I'd forgotten about our snowball
Until I heard Ruthie shout:
MAXXXX! IT'S MEL-L-L-LLLTING!

And there I spotted our snowball.
By then it was 6:08.
It was now completely melted,
Just a puddle sitting on the plate:
DRIP! DRIP! DRIP!

So now we have no snowball.
It's gone, to our great sorrow.
Perhaps we'll make another,
And let it melt again tomorrow!
HOO-RAY!

Mega-Funny Math Poems & Problems Scholastic Professional Books

Name _____

The Snowball

Our snowball is gone. It's sad but true.
But here is something you can do.
Solve these problems, one by one.
We think you'll have a lot of fun.

SOLVE If you need more space, use a second sheet of paper.

1. How much time passed between when Ruth put the snowball on the dish and the kids had a snack?

_____

2. Ruth and Max ate their snack for 30 minutes. What time was it when they finished their snack?

_____

3. Ruth and Max just finished their snack. In how many minutes would it be 11 o'clock?

_____

4. How much time passed between when Ruth put the snowball on the dish and the kids came back from walking the dog?

_____

5. How much time passed between finishing the snack and finishing the dog walk?

_____

6. How much time passed from 8 past 3 o'clock until Ruth and Max finished playing monster games?

_____

7. How long did it take the snowball to melt?

_____

SUPER CHALLENGE Take an ice cube out of the freezer. How long does it take to melt? Use a clock to find out.

_____

How could you make a clock with ice cubes? Explain your method. How would your clock be different from other clocks?

_____

_____

_____

_____

_____

_____

Suds

My name is Max,
I'm nine and a half.
I'm a pretty clean kid,
So why take a bath?

I ask this same question
Every night at seven-thirty:
Why do I need a bath
If I'm NOT really all that dirty?

How can I explain that
When it comes to dirt, you see,
I sort of get attached to it,
And it gets attached to me!

So why should I scrub?
Why should I soak?
The whole thing is ridiculous,
The whole thing is a joke.

Why wash my ears?
Why wash my hair?
I'm tired of all that washing,
I just don't think it's fair.

Oh, I know what they will say
And try as hard as I might,
I just don't believe in taking baths—
I just don't think it's right.

And so when I grow up,
Here's what I will do:
I'll take a bath maybe once a week
Or possibly every two!

Wait—why not every month?
Or maybe every year?
At midnight on the 4th of July
If the weather's cool and clear.

Mega-Funny Math Poems & Problems   Scholastic Professional Books

Name _____

Suds

Enough about bath time,
Let's start in on math time!

SOLVE If you need more space, use a second sheet of paper.

1. Suppose Max takes a bath once a week starting on Tuesday, December 1. How many baths will he take in the month of December?

_____

2. How many baths will Max take in January if he keeps up the 7-day schedule from problem 1?

_____

3. Will Max take a bath on his birthday, January 26? If not, how close will he be from his last bath?

_____

4. Starting on February 1, Max will take a bath every 10 days instead of every week. How many baths will he take in February?

_____

5. If Max continues his 10-day schedule, on what date will Max take his final bath in February?

_____

6. If Max continues his 10-day schedule, on what date will Max take his first bath in March?

_____

7. Suppose Max switches to a 30-day schedule on April 1. How many baths will he take in April? In May?

_____

8. Max took a bath on August 20, September 3, and September 17. What kind of schedule is he on?

_____

SUPER CHALLENGE The weather has been "cool and clear" at midnight on the 4th of July only five times in the past 20 years. At this rate, how often should Max expect to take a bath?

_____

_____

_____

Zeke and Zack

Hello everyone,
This is Max. I'm back!
And this is the tale
Of Zeke and Zack.

Yes, Zack and Zeke,
Zeke and Zack,
Two great friends,
A dog and a cat.

They ran away,
This dog and this kitty.
Soon they were gone,
Lost in the city.

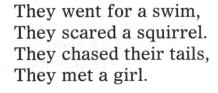

Zeke was big,
And Zack was little.
But whatever they found
They split down the middle.

They howled and yowled,
They jumped and flew.
They found a sandwich,
They split it in two.

They found 6 hot dogs
And this worked best:
Zeke took half,
Zack took the rest.

They snuffled and sniffed
All over the town.
They found 10 cheeseburgers,
And scarfed them down.

They passed the zoo,
They saw a giraffe.
They found 9 marshmallows
And each took half.

They went for a swim,
They scared a squirrel.
They chased their tails,
They met a girl.

Her name was Ruthie.
They made her laugh.
She gave them a bone,
They split it in half.

They ran around,
They played 12 games.
Then Ruthie asked them,
"What are your names?"

Zeke and Zack,
Zack and Zeke,
They barked and purred,
But they couldn't speak.

Ruthie said, "Come."
She took them home.
And that, my friends,
Is the end of this poem.

Yes, Zeke was big,
And Zack was little.
But whatever they found,
They split down the middle.

Mega-Funny Math Poems & Problems   Scholastic Professional Books

Name _____

Zeke and Zack

I snuffled and sniffed for math problems
All over town.
So find the answers
And write them down.

SOLVE If you need more space, use a second sheet of paper.

1. Zeke and Zack each took half of the six hot dogs they found. Draw a picture of the hot dogs. Color Zeke's red and Zack's blue. How many did each get?

2. Draw the 10 cheeseburgers that Zeke and Zack found. Color Zeke's red and Zack's blue. How many did each get?

3. Draw the bone that Ruthie gave to Zeke and Zack. Color Zeke's half red. Color Zack's half blue.

4. Draw a rectangle. Divide it into four parts. What fraction is each part?

5. Suppose Zeke and Zack split the rectangle in problem 4 into two parts. How many parts does Zeke get? How many of the 4 parts does Zack get?

_____

6. Draw another rectangle. Divide it so Zeke, Zack, and Ruthie get equal parts. What fraction does each of them get?

7. Draw nine marshmallows. Divide them into 3 equal groups. What fraction does each group represent? How many marshmallows are in each group?

SUPER CHALLENGE How can Zeke and Zack split 9 marshmallows in half? How many marshmallows will each get?

_____

_____

_____

Modeling Fractions

The Six Days of Summer Vacation

Sung to the tune of "The Twelve Days of Christmas"

Hi, my name is Ruth, and it's time
For our song sing-a-bration.
Would you like to sing a song,
In a voice that's loud and strong,
Called "The Six Days of Summer Vacation"?

On the first day of vacation,
My friend Max gave to me
One ridiculous fractional poem,
And one-half
Of the giraffes
That you see.

On the second day of vacation,
My friend Max gave to me
One ridiculous fractional poem,
Half of the giraffes,
And two-thirds
Of the birds
On this tree.

On the third day of vacation,
My friend Max gave to me
One ridiculous fractional poem,
Half of the giraffes,
Two-thirds of the birds,
And three-fourths
Of a horse
Named Emily.

On the fourth day of vacation,
My friend Max gave to me
One ridiculous fractional poem,
Half of the giraffes,
Two-thirds of the birds,
Three-fourths of the horse,
And four-fifths
Of the ships
In the sea.

On the fifth day of vacation,
My friend Max gave to me
One ridiculous fractional poem,
Half of the giraffes,
Two-thirds of the birds,
Three-fourths of the horse,
Four-fifths of the ships,
And five-sixths
Of the baby chicks
That say "cheep!"

Mega-Funny Math Poems & Problems   Scholastic Professional Books

The Six Days of Summer Vacation

On the sixth day of vacation
You can COLOR everything.
...half of the giraffes.
...two-thirds of the birds.
...three-fourths of the horse.
...two-fifths of the ships.
...five-sixths of the chicks.
And when you're done
Send it to Ruthie and me.

SOLVE

1. How many giraffes do you see in the picture? How many giraffes did Max give to Ruth? Color the giraffes that Max gave to Ruth green.

2. How many birds do you see in the picture? How many birds did Max give to Ruth? Color these birds blue. What fraction of the birds are blue?

_____

3. Color the part of the horse that Max gave to Ruth red. What fraction shows the part of the horse that is red?

_____

4. Color the ships that Max gave to Ruth orange. What fraction of the ships are orange?

_____

5. Color the chicks that Max gave to Ruth yellow. What fraction of the chicks are yellow?

_____

6. Ruth had 6 cars. She gave 4 of them to Max for a gift. What fraction of the cars did Ruth give to Max? Write the fraction in simplest form.

_____

7. Ruth had 12 cars. She gave 9 of them to Max for a gift. What fraction of the cars did Ruth give to Max? Write the fraction in simplest form.

_____

SUPER CHALLENGE Which is more—$\frac{1}{2}$ of 20, or $\frac{2}{3}$ of 15? Explain your answer.

_____

_____

_____

_____

_____

Why?

Hello, my name is Max,
I'm a curious kind of guy.
I have a lot of questions,
And they all begin with *Why*.

For example, here's a sample
Of some things I'd like to know.
It's just a start, but in my heart
I know this list will grow.

Why does $\frac{1}{2}$ equal $\frac{3}{6}$?
Why is the ocean blue?
Why can't you teach old dogs new tricks?
Why is a lie untrue?

Why do stars twinkle and laundry wrinkle?
Why are two halves all?
Why do flowers grow and the wind blow?
Why is a giraffe so tall?

Why is me the opposite of you?
Why is x the unknown?
Why does $\frac{8}{4}$ equal 2?
And why does a dog like a bone?

Why is $\frac{5}{8}$ more than $\frac{1}{2}$?
And why is dust so dirty?
Why can't I fly like a bird?
Why does 10 equal $\frac{1}{3}$ of 30?

Why do chickadees cheep and lizards leap?
Why don't sideburns smoke?
Why do monkeys chatter and pancake batter?
Why don't crocuses croak?

Why does $\frac{9}{12}$ equal $\frac{3}{4}$?
Why do ducks like to float?
Why is south the opposite of north?
Why don't kids get to vote?

Why do crickets chirp and bullfrogs burp?
Why don't dandelions roar?
Why does the moon shine and Franken stein?
Why do eagles soar?

Mega-Funny Math Poems & Problems   Scholastic Professional Books

Name _____

Why?

Why do flowers bloom and rockets zoom?
Why is the sun so high?
Why are hamsters small, but most of all,
Why do I always ask **why?**

SOLVE If you need more space, use a second sheet of paper.

1. Why is $\frac{1}{2}$ equal to $\frac{3}{6}$? Draw a picture to explain.

2. Write three other fractions that are also equal to $\frac{1}{2}$.

_____

3. Write two fractions that are equal to 1. Write two fractions that are equal to 2.

_____

4. Explain why $\frac{5}{8}$ is greater than $\frac{1}{2}$. Draw a picture to explain.

5. Write these fractions in order from largest to smallest: $\frac{1}{2}$, $\frac{5}{6}$, $\frac{7}{8}$, $\frac{3}{4}$.

_____

6. What is the lowest common denominator of the fractions $\frac{1}{4}$ and $\frac{1}{6}$?

_____

7. What is the sum of $\frac{1}{4}$ and $\frac{1}{6}$? What is the difference between $\frac{1}{4}$ and $\frac{1}{6}$?

_____

_____

8. Which of these sums is greater than 1: $\frac{1}{5} + \frac{1}{4}$ or $\frac{5}{6} + \frac{1}{2}$? How can you tell by estimating?

_____

_____

_____

SUPER CHALLENGE The sum of $\frac{1}{4}$, $\frac{1}{3}$, and what other fraction is exactly equal to 1?

_____

Mega-Funny Math Poems & Problems Scholastic Professional Books

Equivalent Fractions • Adding Fractions • Ordering Fractions

TV Guide

My name is Ruth,
And here is my list
Of favorite TV programs
And shows that can't be missed.

Now Monday night has football,
But it's not my cup of tea.
There are just too many commercials,
And it's on too late for me.

Tuesday's full of comedies,
And what a scream they are.
But Tuesday is the day
I like to practice my guitar.

Wednesdays they have talk shows,
Oh, the blabber of it all!
So Wednesday is my day
To go out and play some ball.

Thursdays they have news shows,
Which are really worth a look.
But Thursday is my day
To catch up on reading books.

Friday's full of kids' shows,
And some are really great.
But Friday is my day
To go out and roller-skate.

Saturday cartoons go on and on,
You think they'll never end.
But why stay home and sit
When you can go out and play with friends?

On Sunday there are movies,
And some I really like.
But I'd rather spend the day
With my dog out on a hike.

Mega-Funny Math Poems & Problems   Scholastic Professional Books

Name _____

TV Guide

So that's my TV week—
It's terrific, as I've said.
But I guess I'd really rather
Just do something else instead!

SOLVE If you need more space, use a second sheet of paper.

1. Ruth practiced her guitar for $\frac{1}{4}$ of an hour on Monday and $\frac{1}{2}$ of an hour on Tuesday. In all, what fraction of an hour did Ruth practice?

_____

2. Ruth started reading her book on Thursday. She read $\frac{1}{4}$ of the book before dinner and $\frac{1}{6}$ of the book after dinner. What fraction of the book did she read in all?

_____

3. What fraction of the book is left for Ruth to read in problem 2?

_____

4. Ruth played outside for $2\frac{3}{8}$ hours on Friday and $1\frac{3}{4}$ hours on Saturday. How long did she play in all?

_____

5. How much longer did Ruth play on Friday than on Saturday in problem 4?

_____

6. A TV show lasted $\frac{1}{2}$ hour. Ruth watched $\frac{2}{3}$ of the show. What fraction of an hour did she watch?

_____

7. Ruth missed $\frac{5}{6}$ of a TV show that lasted $1\frac{1}{2}$ hours. How many minutes did she miss?

_____

8. A one-hour TV movie had 6 sets of commercials that lasted $1\frac{2}{3}$ minutes each. How many total minutes of commercials did the show have? What fraction of the show was commercials?

_____

_____

SUPER CHALLENGE How much Empty Time do you have in your day? Find the total amount of Empty Time by adding: (a) the time you are asleep and (b) the time you watch TV. What fraction of your day is Empty Time?

_____

Adding, Subtracting, and Multiplying Fractions and Whole Numbers

Soup's On!

My name is Ruth,
And this is the scoop.
Max and I
Are making some soup.

Our recipe starts
With a heavy iron pot.
We dump in 8 quarts of water,
Then heat until it's hot.

And when the stuff starts boiling,
We add sticks and stones,
A pint of pickled pebbles,
And a pound of octopus bones.

We stir in 12 ounces of mud
And a gob of greasy gizzards,
A half gallon of grimy grit
And the horns of 20 lizards.

To that we add licorice
And some broken bicycle spokes,
Then we turn up the heat
Until the stuff really starts to smoke.

And then when it's finally ready,
We get out the dishes.
What a mouth-watering mix!
Oh, it looks *so* delicious!

But as you may have guessed,
While the mix is heating,
This soup is fun to make,
But it's *not* so great for eating.

Mega-Funny Math Poems & Problems Scholastic Professional Books

Name _____

Soup's On!

So if you want something
For your hunger or your thirst,
Then please don't use our recipe
'Cause our soup is just the worst!

SOLVE If you need more space, use a second sheet of paper.

1. The soup contains 8 quarts of water. Each quart has 32 ounces. How many ounces of water is this?

_____

2. A bowl contains 288 ounces of soup. How many quarts is this?

_____

3. Each quart has 2 pints. How many pints are in 12 quarts? 9 quarts?

_____

_____

4. How many ounces are in one pint?

_____

5. A gallon has 4 quarts. How many pints are in a gallon?

_____

6. How many ounces are in a gallon? (Remember: Each quart has 32 ounces.)

_____

7. Each quart has 4 cups. How many cups are in one gallon?

_____

8. Which is more—9 cups or $2\frac{1}{2}$ quarts? How much more?

_____

_____

9. Think of three different ways to make a gallon using cups, pints, and quarts.

_____

_____

_____

MEASUREMENT CHART

1 quart	=	32 ounces
1 quart	=	2 pints
1 quart	=	4 cups
1 gallon	=	4 quarts

Morrie's Thanksgiving Tale

My name is Ruth
And this is the story
Of a boy I know
Whose name was Morrie.
He was the boy who *always wanted more . . .*

One Thanksgiving day,
on November twenty-third,
When Morrie's friends and family
Sat down to eat their bird,
Instead of being thankful,
This is what occurred:
Morrie cried, *"I want more!"*

They filled Morrie's plate,
but he demanded more food.
He kept on shouting "More!"
This was even when he chewed.
"I'm sorry," Morrie said,
"If you think I'm being rude.
But I absolutely *must have more!"*

They gave him 8.6 kg,
but he wanted 10.2.
And when he tried to eat it all
He started turning blue.
They asked him, "Are you done?"
But he said, "I'm still not through!
You see, I really *must have more!"*

Finally Morrie saw that
if he ate another drop,
He'd be so full of food
That he'd absolutely pop.
So for the first time ever,
Morrie simply shouted, "STOP!
I don't really want any more."

Mega-Funny Math Poems & Problems   Scholastic Professional Books

Name _____

Morrie's Thanksgiving Tale

> From that day on things changed,
> As by now you may have guessed.
> Morrie still wants more sometimes,
> And sometimes he wants less.
> So THIS year on Thanksgiving,
> What do YOU think would be best?
> Should Morrie have more—or less?

SOLVE If you need more space, use a second sheet of paper.

1. Write the number of kilograms of food that *you* think Morrie should eat this Thanksgiving. Is it more than the 8.6 kilograms he had last year, or less? How much more or less?

_____

2. For Thanksgiving, Morrie's family cooked two turkeys that weighed 9.7 kg and 11.3 kg. What was the total weight of both turkeys?

_____

3. What was the difference in weight between the two turkeys in problem 2?

_____

4. Before cooking, a sweet potato weighed in at 0.3 kg. After cooking, it weighed 0.15 kg. What was the change in weight?

_____

5. Which weighs more—a turnip that weighs 0.2 kg or a turnip that weighs 0.175 kg? How much more?

6. A turkey should be cooked for 30 minutes for each kilogram it weighs. To the nearest half hour, how long would it take to cook an 11.3 kg turkey?

_____

7. Morrie's dad arranged four carrots by length from shortest to longest. Their lengths were: 9.65 cm, 9.07 cm, 9.1 cm, and 9.7 cm. List the carrots by length.

_____

_____

8. What length would the carrots in problem 7 reach if they were lined up end to end?

_____

SUPER CHALLENGE How could you make all the carrots in problem 7 the same size? How much would you need to cut from the end of each carrot?

_____

_____

Adding, Subtracting, and Ordering Fractions

The Deci-Mator

My name is Max-dot-Maddux.
Have your decimals lost their step?
Do they just sit there lifelessly,
Without any dash or pep?

Then try my brand-new Deci-Mator,
It's quite an amazing device.
It'll outperform your current machine,
Or we'll refund you 10 TIMES the price!

Yes, the Deci-Mator is amazing,
With its turbo-magnetic chip.
It'll take your worn-out decimals
And fill them with vigor and zip!

Take a number like 1.7,
And stuff it into the machine.
It'll come out worth 10 times as much
And be smoother and spotlessly clean.

Or try a whole number like 20,
And drop it into the Deci-Mator.
It'll come out worth 200—
In other words, 10 times greater!

Does your family have smaller decimals?
Are you in for a surprise!
Turn the Deci-Mator dial to 100,
And watch them balloon in size!

Or what about oversized decimals,
Do they cause you unneeded stress?
Turn the Deci-Mator dial to the left,
And instead of more, they're worth less!

Mega-Funny Math Poems & Problems   Scholastic Professional Books

Name _____

The Deci-Mator

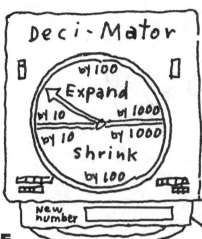

Yes, order your very own Deci-Mator,
The amazing decimal device
That multiplies things by powers of 10,
Including its very own price!

SOLVE

1. Suppose you put the number 3 into the Deci-Mator and turned the dial to expand by the power of 10. What number would come out?

_____

2. What number would come out if you put 4.6 into the Deci-Mator and expanded it 100 times?

_____

3. Use the Deci-Mator to expand 54.3 1000 times. What number do you get?

_____

4. Use the Deci-Mator to shrink 54.3 10 times. What number do you get?

_____

5. Max put the number 62.3 into the Deci-Mator and 623 came out. What setting was the machine on?

_____

6. Ruth put the number 37.44 into the Deci-Mator and 0.3744 came out. What setting was the machine on?

_____

7. What setting would you need to put the machine on to shrink the number 954 to less than 1?

_____

SUPER CHALLENGE Max put 42.3 in the Deci-Mator. First he shrunk the number. Then he shrunk the result again. Then he expanded it twice and shrunk it again. He ended up with the same number he started with—42.3. What settings did Max use for each of these steps?

_____

_____

_____

_____

Playing Percentages

I'm 90 percent positive
That my head's attached to my neck.
On second thought, I'm not so sure—
Perhaps I'd better check!

I'm 17 percent convinced
That crocodiles are bashful and shy.
Why else would they be so quiet
And never say hello or good-bye?

I'm 51 percent sure
That cheese is delicious to eat.
Though sometimes it gets kind of moldy
And smells like somebody's feet.

I'm 83 percent confident
That June comes *after* July.
You just have to be patient and wait
Until 11 months pass by.

I'm 36 percent sure
That *now* comes just before *then*.
But sometimes I get confused—
I'm not sure exactly when!

I'm 80 percent positive
That dogs don't know how to talk.
But sometimes I have my doubts,
When it's time to go for a walk.

I'm 30 percent certain
That someday will never arrive.
But we keep getting closer to it
Each day that we are alive.

Mega-Funny Math Poems & Problems   Scholastic Professional Books

Name_____

Playing Percentages

I'm 100 percent sure
That if you do these problems today,
Your head will stay attached to your neck
At least for another day!

SOLVE If you need more space, use a second sheet of paper.

1. Max is 90 percent sure that his head is attached to his neck. Ninety percent means the same as what number out of 100?

_____

2. Write 90 percent as a fraction and a decimal. Write the fraction in its simplest form.

_____

3. Max is 51 percent sure that cheese is delicious to eat. Is he more than half sure or less than half sure? Explain.

_____

_____

_____

4. Write 50 percent as a fraction and a decimal. Write the fraction in simplest form.

_____

_____

5. Which percents in the poem are greater than half? Which are less than half?

_____

6. Max saw 8 crocodiles. Fifty percent of the crocodiles were asleep. How many crocodiles were asleep?

_____

7. Twenty dogs played in the park. Thirty percent of the dogs were on a leash. Fifty percent were running free. The rest of the dogs were asleep. How many dogs were on a leash, running free, and asleep?

_____

SUPER CHALLENGE Sixty percent of an unknown number is equal to 18. What is the unknown number?

_____

Bicycle Max

My name is Max—
Max A. Maddux if you like
But don't bother me now,
'Cause I'm riding my bike.

I'm the world's greatest rider,
I can ride on any street.
I can ride with just one hand,
I can ride without my feet.

There's just one small problem,
Can you imagine how I feel?
To be the greatest rider ever
But still ride with training wheels!

I tried to take them off,
But this is what I found:
After wobbling back and forth,
I ended up falling down.

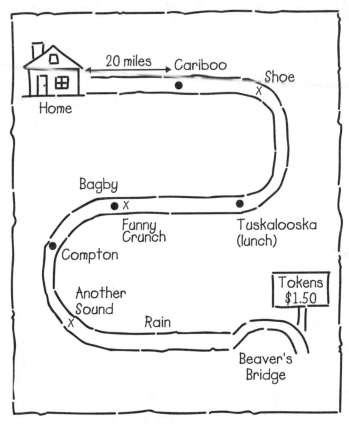

I must admit it bothers me,
It really cramps my style.
So to make up for it,
I ride for miles and miles.

I rode for 20 miles
To a town called Cariboo.
Then I rode for 16 miles before
I stopped to tie my shoe.

I rode to Tuskalooska,
Then I stopped for lunch.
I was 2 miles outside of Bagby
When I heard a funny crunch.

I was 15 miles past Compton
When I heard another sound.
I was going down a hill,
So I could not turn around.

For 18 miles it rained,
Then both my tires popped.
My handlebars came loose,
But there was still no place to stop.

Finally, at Beaver's Bridge,
I saw my brakes were broken.
So I shot into the air—
I didn't even have a token!

I sailed right over everything,
Then crashed onto a lawn.
When I looked at my bike I saw
My training wheels were gone!

"Oh wow!" I cried, "I did it!
Can you imagine how it feels?
I'm still the greatest rider,
But now I DON'T need training wheels!"

Mega-Funny Math Poems & Problems   Scholastic Professional Books

Name _____

Bicycle Max

There's just one thing,
When you're reading this poem,
Don't try any of Max's tricks
On your own bikes at home!

SOLVE Use the information in the poem and the map to solve the problems.

1. What is the distance from where Max started to the place where he stopped to tie his shoe?

_____

2. The distance from Cariboo to Tuskalooska is 40 miles. How far is Tuskalooska from home?

_____

3. The distance from Tuskalooska to Bagby is 24 miles. How far is from Tuskalooska to the place where Max heard the "funny crunch"?

_____

4. The distance from Bagby to Compton is 16 miles. How far is it from home to Compton?

_____

5. The distance from Compton to Beaver's Bridge is 9 miles less than the distance from home to Tuskalooska. (See problem 2.) How far is it from Compton to Beaver's Bridge?

_____

6. What is the entire distance from Home to Beaver's Bridge?

_____

7. If tokens cost $1.50 each way, how many round-trips could you make across Beaver's Bridge for $25?

_____

SUPER CHALLENGE There is a store halfway between Bagby and Cariboo. How far is it from Bagby?

_____

Hoop Dreams

Hey there, fans of basketball,
Is playing hoop your dream?
I'm Ruth, this is Max,
And it's time to meet our team.

We call our squad the Grasshoppers,
We're really not that great.
We've won exactly 3 ball games
And lost some 28!

We're not very good at dribbling,
Our passes have no spin.
Our shots all look good going out,
But very few go in.

We're not very good at rebounding,
We're not quick on our feet.
But when it comes to keeping score,
Us Hoppers can't be beat.

Like take the other day
Against the Kangaroos.
Our team made 13 baskets
While they made 32.

"We're creaming you!" the Roos cried.
"We're winning, we've got more!"
"It's true," we said. "You are ahead.
But do you know the score?"

For if you count 2 points
For every shot you make
And add 1 point for free throws
Keeping score's a piece of cake.

 *Mega-Funny Math Poems & Problems* Scholastic Professional Books

⊕ ⊖ ⊗ ⊘ ⊜ ⊕ ⊖ ⊗ ⊘ **PROBLEM SOLVING**

Hoop Dreams

Since we made 5 free throws
And the Roos made 24,
Can you total all the points
And figure out the score?

SOLVE If you need more space, use a second sheet of paper.

1. How many points do the Hoppers have?

_____

2. How many points do the Roos have? Which team won the game? By how many points?

_____

_____

3. How many games will the Hoppers need to win in a row to have the same number of wins and losses?

_____

4. What will the Hoppers win-lose record be if they win 10 out of the next 15 games?

_____

5. Ruth scored 8 two-point baskets, 4 three-point baskets, and 5 free throws. How many total points did she score?

_____

6. Max scored a total of 16 points. If he made 4 free throws and no three-pointers, how many two-pointers did he make?

_____

7. Ralph, the captain of the Roos, scored 31 points on two-pointers and three-pointers. If he made 5 two-pointers, how many three-pointers did he make?

_____

8. In the play-offs, Max and Ruth each scored 24 points. Max made all his points on two-pointers. Ruth made all her points on three-pointers. Who made more baskets? How many more?

_____

SUPER CHALLENGE Find six different ways that a player can score 10 points in a game.

_____

_____

Mega-Funny Math Poems & Problems   Scholastic Professional Books

King for a Day

My name is Max—I'm nine and a half,
And here's what I have to say:
I'd like to be named king of the world,
If just for one single day.

King Max the First I'd call myself,
I'd wear a royal crown.
And if you wanted to speak to me,
You'd have to kneel down.

I'd pass some great new laws
And enforce them on the spot.
Like people have to play video games
Whether they like them or not.

Or if you didn't play video games,
You'd do something else instead.
Like sit around and read chapter books
And never get out of bed!

No one would ever be bored in my kingdom,
No one would ever be tired.
And if you ever did too much work,
Guess what—I'd have you fired!

I'd deck the halls with potato chips,
And put pizza on every table.
I'd pour root beer out of every faucet,
And every TV would have cable.

I'd get rid of all traffic jams,
Get rid of all cars and trucks.
I'd give everyone a pony to ride,
And a check for a million bucks.

Mega-Funny Math Poems & Problems   Scholastic Professional Books

Name _____

King for a Day

Yes, that's what I'd do if I were king,
And I'm not ashamed to say
The world would be a much better place
If just for one single day.

SOLVE

1. Suppose Max the First gave you a check for one million dollars. If you spent $10,000 per day, how long would it take you to spend your million?

_____

2. Suppose you spent $50,000 a day. If you started spending on May 1, on what date would you have spent the entire million dollars?

_____

3. Three gallons of root beer pour out of Max's faucets every 2 minutes. How long would it take to fill a 90-gallon bucket?

_____

4. By law, citizens of Max's kingdom must play at least 15 hours of video games each month. On average, how long do they need to play each day?

_____

5. Workers in Max's kingdom must work 15 minutes out of every hour. The rest of the time they goof off. How many hours would it take a worker actually to work for 60 minutes?

_____

6. A worker in problem 5 was at her job for 8 hours. How many hours did she goof off? How many hours did she work?

_____

7. Max's pony traveled at a speed of 12 miles per hour. Could the pony travel 70 miles in fewer than 6 hours? Explain using an estimate.

_____

_____

_____

8. The world's most expensive car costs $180,000. Use estimation to find the number of cars you could buy with one million dollars.

_____

SUPER CHALLENGE Suppose you got one million dollars in 100-dollar bills. How many 100-dollar bills would you have in all?

_____

_____

Max and the Millions

My name is Max, I'd like to say "Hi."
Music is my life, I'm a rock-and-roll guy.
The name of my band is Max and the Millions.
We're not famous now, but someday we'll make zillions.

Ruthie will play drums, I'll play guitar.
I'll wear a golden costume, they'll call me Superstar.
We'll sing on MTV, we'll play on radio.
And for only 39 dollars, you can come and see our show.

We'll have laser lights, fireworks, holograms, and more,
State-of-the-art computers, special effects galore!
We'll tour the U.S.A: Max and the Millions Live!
Buy a souvenir T-shirt—only $14.95!

Fans? We won't forget 'em. Autographs are free.
Please include $16.50 (postage and handling fee).
And join Max's fan club—only $18.99.
Visit our virtual Web site—the Millions are on-line!

Mega-Funny Math Poems & Problems Scholastic Professional Books

Name _____

Max and the Millions

So if you'll please excuse us, we need to practice now.
Did I mention playing instruments? (We really don't know how!)
And we need to make up songs—just how hard could that be?
For a group of genuine superstars—Ruth, the Millions . . . and me!

SOLVE   Use estimation when possible.

1. How many $39 tickets for the Max and the Millions show can you buy for $200? For $150?

2. How many ten-dollar bills would you need to buy a ticket to the show, an autograph, and a T-shirt?

3. Which would cost more—4 T-shirts or 3 fan-club memberships?

4. A fan spent exactly $75.96 on four items. Did she buy 4 T-shirts, 4 fan-club memberships, or 4 autographs?

5. A dozen T-shirts have a special price of $175. How much do you save over the regular price?

6. A fan spent exactly $72.00 on a ticket and two items. Which items did he buy?

7. Suppose you had $50. Think of five different ways you could spend your money on Max and the Millions merchandise. Include autographs, fan-club memberships, T-shirts, or tickets.

8. How many different ways could you spend $100 on Max and the Millions tickets and autographs?

SUPER CHALLENGE   Suppose a CD producer offered Max two different deals. In Deal A, the group gets $1 per record and a $10,000 bonus. In Deal B, the group gets $2 per record and a $1,000 bonus. If about 10,000 CDs are sold, which deal is better? Explain.

Dear Max

My name's Max A. Maddux,
Got a problem? Write to me.
I guarantee I'll solve it,
Or your next problem is free!

Like Wanda Petulski,
Of Fort Wayne, who writes:
Dear Max: It's our puppy,
We love him, but he bites.

It's not that it bothers us.
It's not that it hurts.
But this puppy, Dear Max,
Chewed up 36 shirts!

Or take, for example,
When we're not home—
He makes long-distance calls
From our cellular phone!

He ordered 16 pizzas
From Lake Charles, Louisiana.
There's only one thing wrong—
We live in Indiana!

He deprogrammed our computer
And traded in our TV set
For a 10-pound bag of puppy chow
And a kitten named Yvette.

And if you think that's bad,
Without one word of thanks,
He withdrew 775 dollars
Out of five different banks.

So Max, can you help me?
Can you make him mind his manners?
Signed, Wanda Petulski
Of Fort Wayne, Indiana.

Dear Wanda: It is shocking
To hear what your puppy did.
But his problem, as I see it,
Is he thinks he is a KID!

The solution is almost
Too obvious to mention.
Treat your puppy like a DOG—
He wants your attention!

Play some doggy games,
Take a walk, play catch.
Toss an old tennis ball
And say, "Here boy, fetch!"

If that doesn't work,
If he doesn't get better
Then give me a call,
Or write another letter.
    Sincerely,
    Max

Mega-Funny Math Poems & Problems Scholastic Professional Books

Dear Max

SOLVE If you need more space, use a second sheet of paper.

1. Wanda's puppy chewed up 36 shirts. Seventeen of these were T-shirts worth $10 each. The rest were sport shirts that cost $14.95 each. What was the total value of shirts that the puppy ruined?

_____

2. The puppy chewed up twice as many shirts as shoes. How many **pairs** of shoes did he chew?

_____

3. The puppy's bill for 16 pizzas was $264. Each pizza cost $15. The rest of the cost was postage. What was the postage charge for each pizza?

_____

4. The pizza place had 4 different toppings: mushrooms, pepperoni, olives, and sausage. How many different 4-item pizzas are possible? 3-item pizzas?

_____

5. Long-distance calls on the cellular phone cost 95¢ for the first 3 minutes plus 11¢ per minute for calls over 3 minutes. How much would a 4-minute call cost? A 10-minute call?

_____

6. Which costs more—making three calls for 4 minutes each or one call for 23 minutes? How much more?

_____

7. Wanda had a total of $775 in five different banks. She had $200 in one bank. What was the average amount in the remaining 4 banks?

_____

SUPER CHALLENGE In problem 7, Wanda had a total of $775 in five banks. Wanda had twice as much money in the first bank than the second, twice as much in second bank as the third, and so on. If she had $200 in one of the banks, how much did she have in the others?

_____

Answers

The Ice Cream Shop, page 11

1. 50¢, 20¢, 15¢, 8¢
2. 93¢
3. no; 7¢
4. $1.03
5. 3¢
6. 21¢
7. Answers will vary. Typical response: 2 quarters, 2 dimes, 1 nickel, 4 pennies
8. 2 dollar bills; 42¢

SUPER CHALLENGE too much change; she should return 4¢

The Great Card Castle Disaster, page 13

1. See table below.
2. See table below.

SUPER CHALLENGE The pattern is: 6, 6, 7, 7, 8, 8, 9, 9, 10. Students should see that the number of combinations increases by 1 after every even number. See table below.

Square Dance Sing-Along Jubilee, page 15

1. 10
2. $11 - 5 = 6$
3. Answers will vary.
4. Answers will vary.
5. Answers will vary.
6. Possible responses include $36 \div 2 = 18$; $36 \div 3 = 12$; $36 \div 4 = 9$; $36 \div 6 = 6$; $36 \div 9 = 4$

SUPER CHALLENGE Answers will vary.

Bug City, page 17

1. 24
2. 24
3. 16
4. 32
5. 48
6. 30
7. 8
8. 45

SUPER CHALLENGE after 6 days

Number	Ways to Add	Total Number of Ways
10	10 + 0, 9 + 1, 8 + 2, 7 + 3, 6 + 4, 5 + 5	6
11	11 + 0, 10 + 1, 9 + 2, 8 + 3, 7 + 4, 6 + 5	6
12	12 + 0, 11 + 1, 10 + 2, 9 + 3, 8 + 4, 7 + 5, 6 + 6	7
13	13 + 0, 12 + 1, 11 + 2, 10 + 3, 9 + 4, 8 + 5, 7 + 6	7
14	14 + 0, 13 + 1, 12 + 2, 11 + 3, 10 + 4, 9 + 5, 8 + 6, 7 + 7	8
15	15 + 0, 14 + 1, 13 + 2, 12 + 3, 11 + 4, 10 + 5, 9 + 6, 8 + 7	8
16	16 + 0, 15 + 1, 14 + 2, 13 + 3, 12 + 4, 11 + 5, 10 + 6, 9 + 7, 8 + 8	9
17	17 + 0, 16 + 1, 15 + 2, 14 + 3, 13 + 4, 12 + 5, 11 + 6, 10 + 7, 9 + 8	9
18	18 + 0, 17 + 1, 16 + 2, 15 + 3, 14 + 4, 13 + 5, 12 + 6, 11 + 7, 10 + 8, 9 + 9	10

Max's Talent Show, page 19

1. 8
2. 3
3. 108
4. 12
5. 2 less than 50
6. 8
7. $350
8. 3

SUPER CHALLENGE $500. If he takes $35 per show, he will make $35 times 2 shows per day times 7 days per week, for a total of $490. This is less than a flat fee of $500.

Ruth's Mystery Garden, page 21

1. Answers will vary.
2. Answers will vary. Shapes may include such categories as "round," "long," "skinny," "curved," "heart-shaped," and so on.
3. Answers will vary. Other ways to sort include texture, size, vegetables vs. fruits, sweetness, citrus vs. noncitrus, and so on.
4. Answers will vary. Sweet: bananas, nectarines, plums, strawberries, oranges; Nonsweet: potatoes, tomatoes, sugar peas, hot peppers, pumpkins.
5. Answers will vary. Straight rollers: nectarines, plums, oranges, tomatoes; crooked rollers: strawberries, potatoes, hot peppers, pumpkins; no rollers: bananas, sugar peas, hot peppers
6. Answers will vary.
7. Answers will vary.
8. Answers will vary.

SUPER CHALLENGE Answers will vary.

The Tooth, page 23

1. Next: jelly bean. After that: jelly bean, kiss
2. Next 3: lollipop, lollipop, peppermint. Next 6: lollipop, lollipop, peppermint, lollipop, lollipop, peppermint
3. Anwers will vary.
4. Anwers will vary.
5. Three jelly beans are followed by 3 peppermints. Next 4: peppermint, peppermint, peppermint, jelly bean
6. Answers will vary.
7. The seventh figure, a jelly bean, should be deleted.
8. 4; 5

SUPER CHALLENGE 127

Ruth's Fantastical Zoo, page 25

1. Sketches will vary. All sketches should have square hair and a circular head.
2. Sketches will vary. All sketches should include four rectangles.
3. Sketches will vary. All sketches should have oval-shaped bodies and triangular boots.
4. Sketches will vary. All creatures should have star-shaped bodies.
5. Sketches will vary. All creatures should have triangle-shaped mouths and square ears.
6.

7. Cage should be a parallelogram.
8. Drawings will vary.

SUPER CHALLENGE Sketch should be a parallelogram with a diagonal that connects two corners.

The Snowball, page 27

1. 1 hour
2. 10:30
3. 30 minutes
4. 6 hours 8 minutes
5. 5 hours 8 minutes
6. 2 hours 3 minutes
7. 9 hours 8 minutes

SUPER CHALLENGE Answers will vary. Students should recognize that they can use the length of time it takes ice to melt as a unit to keep track of time.

Suds, page 29

1. 5
2. 4
3. yes
4. 3
5. February 21
6. March 3
7. 1 bath in April; 2 baths in May
8. 1 bath every 14 days

SUPER CHALLENGE 1 bath every 4 years

Zeke and Zack, page 31

1. 3. Drawing should show 3 red and 3 blue hot dogs.
2. 5. Drawing should show 5 red and 5 blue cheeseburgers.
3. Drawing should show a bone that is half red and half blue.
4. $\frac{1}{4}$. Drawing should show a rectangle divided in 4 equal parts.
5. 2 parts each
6. $\frac{1}{3}$. Drawing should show a rectangle divided into 3 equal parts.

7. Each group has 3 marshmallows and represents $\frac{1}{3}$. Drawing should show 9 marshmallows divided into 3 groups of 3 each.

SUPER CHALLENGE Each will get $4\frac{1}{2}$ marshmallows.

The Six Days of Summer Vacation, page 33

1. 2 giraffes; 1 green giraffe
2. 3 birds; 2 birds; $\frac{2}{3}$ are blue
3. $\frac{3}{4}$
4. $\frac{4}{5}$
5. $\frac{5}{6}$
6. $\frac{2}{3}$
7. $\frac{3}{4}$

SUPER CHALLENGE The same; both equal 10.

Why?, page 35

1. Picture should show that $\frac{3}{6}$ and $\frac{1}{2}$ cover an equal area of a circle or other figure.
2. Answers will vary. Typical response: $\frac{2}{4}$, $\frac{3}{6}$, $\frac{4}{8}$
3. Answers will vary. Typical response for 1: $\frac{2}{2}$, $\frac{3}{3}$. For 2: $\frac{2}{1}$, $\frac{4}{2}$
4. One-half is equal to $\frac{4}{8}$. $\frac{5}{8}$ is greater than $\frac{4}{8}$, so it must be greater than $\frac{1}{2}$.
5. $\frac{7}{8}$, $\frac{5}{6}$, $\frac{3}{4}$, $\frac{1}{2}$
6. 12
7. $\frac{5}{12}$; $\frac{1}{12}$
8. $\frac{5}{6} + \frac{1}{2} > 1$. You can tell because $\frac{5}{6}$ is greater than $\frac{1}{2}$. If you add $\frac{1}{2}$ to it, the sum is greater than 1. $\frac{1}{5}$ and $\frac{1}{4}$ are both smaller than $\frac{1}{2}$ so their sum is less than 1.

SUPER CHALLENGE $\frac{5}{12}$

TV Guide, page 37

1. $\frac{3}{4}$ hour
2. $\frac{5}{12}$
3. $\frac{7}{12}$
4. $4\frac{1}{8}$ hours
5. $\frac{5}{8}$
6. $\frac{1}{3}$
7. 75 minutes
8. 10 min; $\frac{1}{6}$

SUPER CHALLENGE Answers will vary.

Soup's On!, page 39

1. 256
2. 9
3. 24; 18
4. 16
5. 8
6. 128
7. 16
8. $2\frac{1}{2}$ quarts; 1 cup (8 oz) more
9. Answers will vary. Typical answers:
   1 gallon = 3 quarts and 2 pints;
   1 gallon = 2 quarts and 4 pints;
   1 gallon = 12 cups and 1 quart

Morrie's Thanksgiving Tale, page 41

1. Answers will vary.
2. 21 kg
3. 1.6 kg
4. 0.15 kg
5. 0.2 kg; 0.025 more
6. $5\frac{1}{2}$ hours
7. 9.7, 9.65, 9.1, 9.07
8. 37.52 cm

SUPER CHALLENGE Answers will vary. Typical answer: Make all of the carrots equal to the smallest carrot, 9.07 cm. This requires cutting 0.63 cm from the 9.7 cm carrot; 0.58 cm from the 9.65 cm carrot; and 0.03 cm from the 9.1 cm carrot.

The Deci-Mator, page 43

1. 30
2. 460
3. 54,300
4. 5.43
5. Multiply, or expand, by 10.
6. Divide, or shrink, by 100.
7. Divide, or shrink, by 1,000.

SUPER CHALLENGE Answers will vary. Sample response: Max divided by 10, then divided by 10 again. Then he multiplied by 10, multiplied by 100, and finally divided by 10.

Playing Percentages, page 45

1. 90
2. $\frac{90}{100} = \frac{9}{10}$, 0.9
3. More than half sure; 51% is greater than 50% or one-half.
4. $\frac{50}{100} = \frac{1}{2}$, 0.5
5. Greater than half: 90%, 51%, 83%, 80%, 100%; less than half: 17%, 36%, 30%
6. 4
7. 6 on a leash, 10 running free, 4 asleep

SUPER CHALLENGE 30

Bicycle Max, page 47

1. 36 miles
2. 60 miles
3. 22 miles
4. 100 miles
5. 51 miles
6. 151 miles
7. 8

SUPER CHALLENGE 32 miles

Hoop Dreams, page 49

1. 31
2. 88; the Roos won by 57 points
3. 25
4. Won 13, lost 33
5. 33
6. 6
7. 7
8. Max made 4 more baskets.

SUPER CHALLENGE 13 different ways in all: (1) 10 free throws; (2) 8 free throws, 1 two-pointer; (3) 7 free throws, 1 three-pointer; (4) 6 free throws, 2 two-pointers; (5) 5 free throws, 1 three-pointer, 1 two-pointer; (6) 4 free throws, 2 three-pointers; (7) 4 free throws, 3 two-pointers; (8) 3 free throws, 1 three-pointer, 2 two-pointers; (9) 2 free throws, 2 three-pointers, 1 two-pointer; (10) 2 free throws, 4 two-pointers; (11) 1 free throw, 3 three-pointers; (12) 1 free throw, 1 three-pointer, 3 two-pointers; (13) 5 two-pointers

King for a Day, page 51

1. 100 days
2. May 21 (20 days)
3. 60 minutes
4. $\frac{1}{2}$ hour
5. 4 hours
6. 6 hours goofing off, 2 hours working
7. Yes, in 6 hours it would travel $6 \times 12 = 72$ miles. So it would travel 70 miles in less than 6 hours.
8. 5

SUPER CHALLENGE 10,000

Max and the Millions, page 53

1. 5; 3
2. 8
3. 4 T-shirts
4. 4 fan-club memberships
5. $4.40
6. 2 autographs
7. Answers will vary. Typical answers: 1 ticket; 3 autographs; 2 autographs and 1 T-shirt; 3 T-shirts; 1 fan-club membership and 1 autograph
8. 2 ways: 2 tickets, 1 autograph; 1 ticket; 3 autographs

SUPER CHALLENGE Deal B. If 10,000 CDs are sold, the first deal a gives: $10,000 bonus + 10,000 × $1 per CD = $20,000. Deal B gives: $1,000 bonus + 10,000 × $2 per CD = $21,000.

Dear Max, page 55

1. $454.05
2. 9 pairs
3. $1.50
4. 1 four-item pizza; 6 three-item pizzas
5. $1.06; $1.72
6. Three 4-minute calls cost 3¢ more
7. $143.75

SUPER CHALLENGE $400, $200, $100, $50, $25

Notes

Notes

Notes